BLACK VOTER SUPPRESSION
The Fight for the Right to Vote

Dr. Artika R. Tyner

Lerner Publications ◆ Minneapolis

Lerner Publications Company
An imprint of Lerner Publishing Group, Inc.
241 First Avenue North
Minneapolis, MN 55401 USA

For reading levels and more information, look up this title at www.lernerbooks.com.

Library of Congress Cataloging-in-Publication Data

Names: Tyner, Artika R., author.
Title: Black voter suppression : the fight for the right to vote / Artika R. Tyner.
Description: Minneapolis : Lerner Publications, 2021. | Series: The fight for Black rights | Includes bibliographical references and index. | Audience: Ages 8–12 | Audience: Grades 4–6 | Summary: "The right to vote is both a historical and a modern-day issue impacting Black Americans. Discover how this hard-fought right was won, and how efforts to disenfranchise Black voters continue to this day"— Provided by publisher.
Identifiers: LCCN 2020041874 (print) | LCCN 2020041875 (ebook) | ISBN 9781728429663 (library binding) | ISBN 9781728429663 (paperback) | ISBN 9781728429557 (ebook)
Subjects: LCSH: African Americans—Suffrage—History—Juvenile literature. | African Americans—Politics and government—Juvenile literature. | Elections—Corrupt practices—United States—Juvenile literature.
Classification: LCC JK1924 .T96 2021 (print) | LCC JK1924 (ebook) | DDC 324.6089/96073—dc23
LC record available at https://lccn.loc.gov/2020041874
LC ebook record available at https://lccn.loc.gov/2020041875

Manufactured in the United States of America
1 – CG – 12/31/20

Table of Contents

CHAPTER 1

The Fight for Georgia 4

CHAPTER 2

The History of Voter Suppression. 10

CHAPTER 3

Modern-Day Voter Suppression 16

CHAPTER 4

Voting In 2020 22

Voting Turnout Demographics 28

Glossary. 30
Learn More 31
Index. 32

THE FIGHT FOR
Georgia

On June 9, 2020, Black Votes Matter cofounder LaTosha Brown waited in a long line to cast her vote in the Georgia primary election. The voting machines in her majority-Black Atlanta neighborhood were not working. Brown ended up waiting three hours before she could vote. Then she drove to assist another voter in a majority-white neighborhood. The contrast between the polling locations was stark. It was a completely different experience. The voting machines were working properly. There were no lines.

During the Georgia primary, the long lines and down voting machines made national news. People were paying special attention after the election for state governor in 2018.

On June 9, 2020, voters in some parts of Atlanta waited in line for more than five hours to cast their votes in the Georgia primary election.

VOTER SUPPRESSION IN GEORGIA

In 2018, Georgia politician Stacey Abrams ran for governor against Brian Kemp. Kemp was Georgia's secretary of state at the time. Part of his job was to oversee state elections— including his own. Under Kemp's watch, Georgia removed over half a million voters from voter rolls in 2017. Kemp's office also blocked 53,000 new voters, most of whom were Black, from registering. Many of the registrations were put on hold because the information on the application did not exactly match the information on file in state databases. Down voting machines, shortages of paper ballots, and long lines on Election Day meant some people had to leave without casting a vote.

About 1.2 million Black voters cast their ballots for Stacey Abrams as governor in 2018.

Stacey Abrams became the first Black woman to run for governor of a US state on a major-party ticket in 2018.

Kemp beat Abrams by a little less than 50,000 votes. It was one of the closest statewide races in recent history. Had all Black votes been counted, there may have been a different result.

WHAT IS BLACK VOTER SUPPRESSION?

Voter suppression is a broad term for any rules or actions
that prevent voters from registering to vote or voting. Voter
suppression can take many forms. It could be that a polling
place runs out of paper ballots before voting ends, or that
eligible voters were unknowingly removed from voter rolls.
Polling places may close or move at the last minute. Voter
registrations may be rejected because of a typo.

In Atlanta, Georgia, more than eighty polling places were closed or combined
ahead of the 2020 primary.

BRIAN KEMP MUST RESIGN

#CantTrustKemp

Many people believed Brian Kemp's run for governor was unethical. He was already the Georgia Secretary of State, and his office was in charge of the election.

Black voter registration increased between 2004 and 2008. Since then, Black voters have faced growing challenges in trying to cast their ballots. But Black voter suppression is not a new issue. Black people have been fighting to protect their voting rights for decades.

? When lines are long, people have to wait for hours to vote. Why might long lines make it hard for someone to vote? How might states or districts try to make voting lines shorter?

CHAPTER 2

THE HISTORY OF
Voter Suppression

The US Civil War lasted from 1861 to 1865. The period immediately afterward is known as Reconstruction. This was a time of rebuilding in America. The Southern Confederate states had surrendered and were rejoining the Union. New amendments to the Constitution meant four million previously enslaved Africans were now free citizens. Federal troops were placed in the former Confederate states to protect the rights of Black people.

More than half a million Black men became voters in the South. They elected officials whose policies helped improve their lives. Around two thousand Black men were elected during Reconstruction. In 1870, Hiram Rhodes Revels was the first Black person to become a US Senator.

Reconstruction ended in 1877, when the troops that had been protecting Black rights were removed. Many Black people were threatened with violence from white supremacists for trying to exercise their voting rights. White supremacists regained control over state legislatures and passed laws to limit the rights of Black people.

Hiram Rhodes Revels is one of only ten Black people to serve in the US Senate. He represented Mississippi, a state that has not elected a Black person to statewide office since 1890.

IT'S THE LAW

States could not legally ban Black people from voting. However, following Reconstruction, states passed Jim Crow laws that led to widespread Black voter suppression.

A political cartoon from 1879 criticizes the use of literacy tests. Even though many white men could not read or write well, they were allowed to vote. Jim Crow laws required Black men to pass a literacy test in order to vote.

Poll taxes were a major barrier to Black voters. Because they were so recently freed from slavery, few had the means to afford the tax. Literacy tests also disenfranchised Black voters. They were given complicated passages to read or asked to answer difficult questions. Often white people were exempt from literacy tests due to the grandfather clause. This clause allowed people to vote if their grandfather could vote before the Civil War. Since the grandfathers of Black people were enslaved and could not vote, they usually could not meet this requirement

Gerrymandering

Gerrymandering is the drawing of district boundaries in an unfair way. Gerrymandering gives one political party an advantage in elections. For example, if Black neighborhoods are chopped into many different districts, they may never be able to elect a politician who supports the Black community. They will not have enough numbers to unite as a group. This is racial gerrymandering.

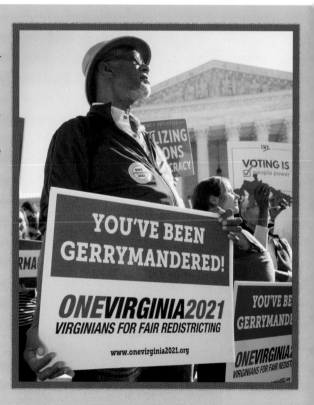

MARCHING FOR THEIR RIGHTS

By 1940, only 3 percent of Black people were registered to vote. The Civil Rights Movement worked to change that. In 1965, Dr. Martin Luther King Jr. organized a march to the courthouse in Selma, Alabama. Hundreds of Black people joined him to register to vote. But they were turned away. King planned another march from Selma to Montgomery, Alabama. Police beat protesters in an attack known as Bloody Sunday. The march was televised and sparked support for Black voting rights.

Dr. Martin Luther King Jr. and other civil rights activists led three protest marches over several weeks. They marched along a 54-mile stretch of highway between Selma and Montgomery.

President Lyndon Johnson *(left)* hands Dr. Martin Luther King Jr. one of the pens used to sign the Voting Rights Act of 1965 into law.

President Lyndon Johnson signed the Voting Rights Act of 1965 to protect Black voting rights. The act made literacy tests illegal and allowed the federal government to challenge the use of poll taxes. Districts that had discriminated against Black voters also had to get federal approval for any changes to their voting laws.

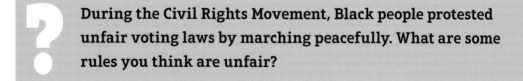

? During the Civil Rights Movement, Black people protested unfair voting laws by marching peacefully. What are some rules you think are unfair?

CHAPTER 3

MODERN-DAY
Voter
Suppression

Voter suppression in the twenty-first century looks different from the past. Some states do not allow voters to register on Election Day. People who were unknowingly purged from voter rolls may not realize that they are no longer registered until they try to vote. At that point, it is too late.

Strict voter ID laws can limit the number of voters. 21 million Americans do not have a photo ID. And in some states, only certain photo IDs are considered acceptable. For example, military IDs may be okay while college IDs are not.

In many states, people convicted of a felony cannot vote. Other states have other laws regarding criminal offenders. In Florida, people who served a prison sentence must pay all court and legal fees before they can vote. This keeps people who don't have very much money from voting.

Elderly Black voters can fall victim to voter suppression if they do not have the correct ID to vote in their state.

Stacey Abrams' Fair Fight is a political action committee dedicated to promoting fair elections around the country, as well as encouraging voter participation.

COUNTING EVERY VOTE

Civil rights groups across the country are working to end voter suppression. Stacey Abrams founded Fair Fight. Its mission is to end voter purges and the need for an exact voter ID match. It also provides information about voting to the community. Abrams is helping Black people vote. Her organization offers a voter protection hotline. Callers can get voting tools and resources.

Celebrities are also helping to fight against Black voter suppression. In 2020, National Basketball Association (NBA) star LeBron James launched More Than a Vote. James partnered with several athletes and artists to create this movement. This includes Kevin Hart and Patrick Mahomes, among many others. Together, they are creating equal access to the ballot box by helping more people in the Black community register to vote. The More Than a Vote website allows people to check if they are registered. If they are not, it helps them register.

Nearly fifty professional athletes and entertainers are founding members of LeBron James's More Than a Vote campaign.

RESTORING THE VOTING RIGHTS ACT

In 2013, the US Supreme Court struck down part of the Voting Rights Act of 1965. The court ruled that the method of choosing which districts must seek federal approval before changing their election policies was unconstitutional.

Civil rights groups such as the National Association for the Advancement of Colored People (NAACP) said the Supreme Court decision could lead to more Black voter suppression.

Disenfranchisement

Black Americans are not the only ones who have issues voting. Forty percent of polling places do not fully accommodate people with disabilities. 21 million US citizens don't have a photo ID. Young and elderly people may not have the correct type of ID. Unhoused people do not have a permanent address, making it more likely their registration will be purged from voter rolls.

INCLUSION! POWER! RIGHTS!

Lily

I have a disability & I WILL VOTE

IndependenceFirst.org

ADA30
Americans with Disabilities Act

independence first

Lawmakers are working to restrengthen voting protections. Forty-eight senators, including Democratic Vice President nominee Kamala Harris, introduced the John Lewis Voting Rights Advancement Act in 2019. The bill would require any state with a history of voter suppression in the past twenty-five years to seek federal approval before making changes that may unfairly affect voters of color.

LeBron James and Stacey Abrams use their influence to inspire others. How can you be a positive influence in your school or community?

VOTING IN
2020

The COVID-19 pandemic has caused many disruptions to voting. People are concerned about the health risks of in-person voting. Many polling stations are closing because they do not have enough volunteer staff. This has raised concerns about voter suppression. In June 2020, a mainly Black county in Kentucky only had one place to vote for more than 750,000 people. Voters had to arrive by 6 p.m. Otherwise, they could not vote. People stood in line for hours. Many could not miss work and were not able to vote.

ElectionS
1-888-742-8
www.electionsou

Due to the 2020 COVID-19 pandemic, the state of Kentucky reduced in-person polling places from more than 3,500 to 170 for the 2020 primary election, which meant many Kentucky residents were not able to vote.

Many politicians from both parties are pushing for mail-in voting, where ballots are sent out to every registered voter. They argue that this will allow people to vote without concerns for their safety, and more voters can participate in states with few polling stations. But delays with the postal service can also cause voter suppression. Many people received their mail-in ballots for the New York June primary at the last minute. It was too late to cast their vote.

In an effort to stop the spread of COVID-19, many states proposed changes to the voting process, including mail-in voting and drop-boxes for paper ballots.

Why the Census Is Important

Every ten years, the US Census counts everyone who lives in the United States. Census numbers are used to help distribute funds for school lunch programs, early education, food assistance, and other programs. The number of representatives each state has in Congress and the number of polling places in a district are determined by Census numbers too. Being counted in the Census helps people in a district access their right to vote.

Many Republicans are against mail-in voting. They say in-person voting reduces voter fraud. Some people fear that voter fraud is a widespread challenge. They suspect that tens of thousands of people may be voting illegally. However, studies show that voter fraud is very rare. A 2014 study showed thirty-one cases of fraud out of one billion votes cast between 2000 and 2014. Some people believe noncitizens are voting. According to the study, suspected noncitizen votes were only 0.0001 percent of votes in the 2016 election.

VOTING IS POWER

The right to vote is an important part of democracy. Elections help to shape laws and policies that in turn impact health care, criminal justice, and education. Elected officials work for the people they represent. Free and fair elections allow people to choose officials that will stand up for their needs.

There are important ways to fight voter suppression and ensure the right to vote for all American people:

1. Stay educated about issues important to you and learn about the candidates.
2. Talk to your parents or guardians about the US Census and voting.
3. Participate in your school's mock election.
4. Watch the news and stay informed on current events and issues.
5. Read the Constitution and learn about the Amendments.

Voter suppression keeps people from voting. Black people have experienced this from slavery to today. What methods could be used to ensure that voting is possible for everyone?

Volunteers with Black Voters Matter went on an eleven-state bus tour across the US to boost Black voter turnout in 2019.

VOTING TURNOUT
Demographics

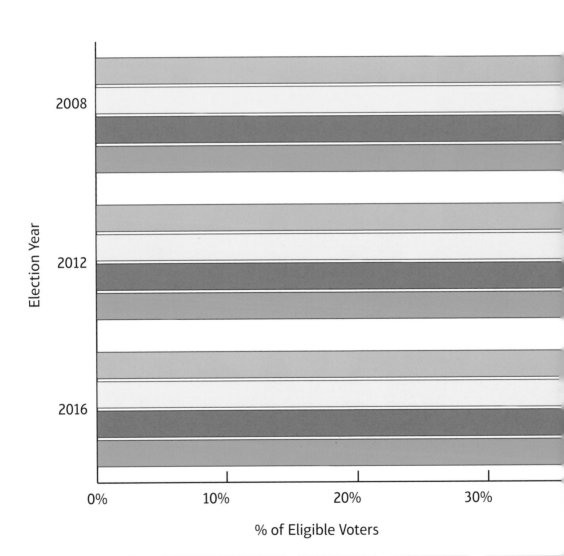

Election Year

2008

2012

2016

0%   10%   20%   30%

% of Eligible Voters

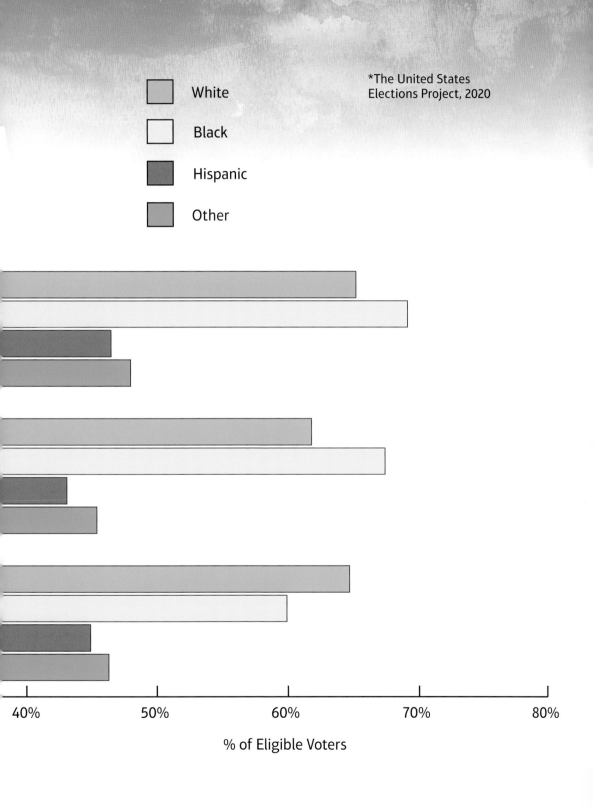

*The United States
Elections Project, 2020

White

Black

Hispanic

Other

40%　　　　50%　　　　60%　　　　70%　　　　80%

% of Eligible Voters

Glossary

enslaved: made into a slave; caused to lose freedom

felon: a person who is convicted of committing a serious crime known as a felony

governor: the elected head of a state

Jim Crow laws: laws used post-Reconstruction to take away the rights of Black people

literacy test: a test of reading ability that a person must pass in order to vote

poll tax: a tax charged to vote

Supreme Court: the highest court in the United States

voter fraud: illegal behavior that could impact the results of an election

voter ID: identification required for voting and voter registration

voter suppression: policies and rules that keep people from being able to vote

white supremacy: the belief that white people are superior and should have control over people of other races, like Black people

Learn More

2020 Census Challenge: United States Census Bureau
https://www.census.gov/library/video/2019/the-2020-census-challenge.html

Fifteenth Amendment: Ducksters
https://www.ducksters.com/history/us_government/fifteenth_amendment.php

Wallace, Sandra Neil. *The Teacher's March! How Selma's Teachers Changed History.* New York: Calkins Creek, 2020.

Westgate, Kathryn. *Landmark Voting Laws.* New York: Gareth Stevens Publishing, 2021.

Voting Rights Act of 1965: History
https://www.history.com/topics/black-history/voting-rights-act

Index

Abrams, Stacey, 6, 7, 18, 21

Black Votes Matter, 4
Bloody Sunday, 14
Brown, LaTosha, 4

Civil War, 10, 13

gerrymandering, 13

Harris, Kamala, 21
Hart, Kevin, 19

James, LeBron, 19, 21
Johnson, Lyndon, 15

Kemp, Brian, 6, 7, 9
King Jr., Dr. Martin Luther, 14, 15

Mahomes, Patrick, 19
mail-in voting, 24, 25
More Than a Vote, 19

polling stations, 22, 24

Revels, Hiram Rhodes, 10, 11

Selma, Alabama, 14

US Census, 25, 26

Voting Rights Act of 1965, 15, 20

Photo Acknowledgments

The images in this book are used with the permission of: Spencer Pratt/
Getty Images, p.5; Jessica McGowan/Getty Images, p.6; Jessica McGowan/
Getty Images, p.7; Matthew Hatcher/Getty Images, p.8; Steve Eberhardt/ZUMA
Wire/Newscom, p.9; MPI/Getty Images, p.11; Library of Congress/Wikimedia,
p.12; Jeff Malet Photography/Newscom, p.13; William Lovelace/Daily Express/
Hulton Archive/Getty Images, p.14; Washington Bureau/Getty Images, p.15;
Michael Bryant/Philadelphia Inquirer/MCT/Newscom, p.17; Bob Andres/Atlanta
Journal-Constitution/TNS/Newscom, p.18; Kevin C. Cox/Getty Images, p.19; Richard
Ellis/Getty Images, p.20; Mark Hertzberg/ZUMA Wire/Newscom, p.21; Brett
Carlsen/Getty Images, p.22; Joe Raedle/Getty Images, p.24; Justin Sullivan/Getty
Images, p.25; Melissa Sue Gerrits/Getty Images, p.27; rosiekeystrokes/Pixabay,
background

Cover: Rowland Sherman/National Archives at College Park/Wikimedia, left;
Jessica McGowan/Getty Images, middle; Mario Tama/Getty Images, right